Gasoline Souls by
Ian Phillips

So we decided to stay together

So we decided to stay together
Not cry and part and regret
Our roads remained conjoined
Not parting towards separate sunsets
We glued that which was broke
Instead of settling debts and gently
handing back keys.
We dived out of the eye of the storm
At first swirling, hands gripping hands
And landed bruised, hurt, damaged
Yet together.

Friday

The end of the week

The day for fish

Clocking off at five

The pay packet in hand

The buzz of the night

Which uncast character

In this unwritten play

Will sing with me?

Red

I like red, not the colour but the word.

I like the word that rhymes with read

And dead, and bed.

I like red as it hides within blood

And its skies at night,

when red, delights men in fields.

I like red for flying the flag

And standing tall

And for staining roses

And bloodied noses.

A day off

As you lie, waiting for a final breath.

Recall that blue-skied day,

When the cool morning sun

Promised fresh river breezes

And oars dipped into honey.

If you have one regret

Don't make it that on that glistening day

Work called out and gripped your soul.

Hobby

Watching TV was his hobby

He learnt all that he spoke about

He told us, from watching TV

Ask me anything he said and I can

Disclose answers as proposed by

Watching all that I have, on TV.

So we asked, one by one

And he answered as he had seen

By watching everything on TV.

And then someone asked,

What does the summer smell like?

And he answered,

That episode hasn't been shown yet

On TV.

Je Ne Regrette Rhiana

It was all taboo

You, me, the world.

Paths crossing at unavoidable times.

And as the moment passed

Falling down like heavy rope,

We grabbed at it

Burning our hands,

Blistering the memories left behind,

That only time's soothing lotion heals.

Eight miles High

Driving through France and thinking

Not of first or second world wars

But of future, of today, of now.

My vision is linked by eight miles of beauty

Holding hands almost, the finger tips swirling

Plucking invisible forms from nowhere

These modern wind catchers are reminders

Of how we should have been.

The Origin of My Species

When I die it will be the start of something

A start of the fading memory of me.

An evaporation of our love

That we carried together and then there was just me.

It will be the start of our children

Untying the boat and pushing us out to sea.

The start of occasional sadness for friends whom we

Can no longer reach

Of repainting walls in our once loved house.

Of pausing over photographs, smiling, smiling.

And while I know lights will be turned off

the origin of my death will be marked,

by that deep reasonance within my children's soul.

What is....

What is your memory of me?

When I was delivered in front of you

That force that had scooped me up

And like a quivering arrow, I landed at your feet.

What is your memory of me?

As my shy drunken eyes

Shone in anticipation.

And our histories remained secret,

Intimacy at the forefront.

What is your memory of me?

As we laugh at our now shared lives.

At our realised unplanned dreams.

At our diluted selves within our children.

At the fears that await us now,

And still your hand feels small in mine.

Each morning..

Each morning I brush my teeth

And stare in the mirror

And remember I am over forty

So cancer fills my mind.

Each morning I reach for slippers

That I haven't bought yet

And rub my back that holds no aches

Yet before long, shall.

Each morning I think

About when I will not be here

And when the theatre curtains draw

Will the exit sign still be burning?

Each morning I awake and smile

And hope for a day of blue skies

Of unplanned laughter

Of days without mourning.

Outsider

Don't bet on me, even experts can't tell.

If I'll fall at the first or stall at the start.

I'll drink til I fall and smoke til fingers yellow,

I'll spike your drink just to get close to you.

I'll watch you from afar measuring every contour,

that rank outsider I have now become.

Yet let me in and I will love you.

With a force reminding you why you are here.

We'll skate across melting rivers,

surf away from land towards burning suns.

And when you are mine and I have defeated your odds.

We'll touch noses and stare deeply into what we have now become.

And our restless hands will grasp out

For the next that will make us whole.

Conversing deflections

Your words bounce off my skin

Grazing, scratching, hurting.

I feel for my weapon

And carefully load in reply.

It's another Valentine's Day slaughter.

You absorb all I fire at you

And there are no exit wounds.

Just another part of you,

Accepting what I am.

I hate..

I hate therefore I am.

I hate that I cannot control fate.

I hate that this plate that I am spinning

Will one day fall.

And when I sleep, these thorns I keep,

Melt into mercury

Cooling my resting soul.

This be The Verve... by Ian Phillips

They sort you out, your mum and dad

Instil you with goodness and ideas

And love.

And they were sorted and loved

By their parents too

In swirling skirts, tanned faces

Fifties, techicolor photographs.

Like a glorious virus we pass on

Our happiness and hope to man.

Revelling, lying in this warm sweet honey,

conjoined by timeless laughter.

Original "This Be The Verse" by Philip Larkin

The problem of Beginning

The problem with a beginning is that there must be an end.

Just as a smile must finally melt,

And an orange sun supplies the closing bracket of a day.

As a celebration draws to a close the end is replaced

By the start of a memory.

Yet goodness comes with endings.

The end of the hike up that steep hill.

The end of the tears and faces pressed into cushions.

The end of a bad day, the end of a frown

The end of waiting, for something like you.

Valerie's getting Old

She's getting old, that Valerie, she said.

Had all her bits pulled up not long back

Now bronchitis is eating her up

It'll just take one thing, then she'll be gone.

This badge of oldness she wears

so forlornly, as she shuffles

staring at her mortal coil.

And then the pause,

The recognition of cool breath on her warmed skin

The glow of sun through closed eyes

That returns her to the calmness of womb.

All I want is all I have

All I want is all I have.

My children to remind me of my good parts.

A lover to patiently mop my ego.

The promise of tomorrow,

without the pain of yesterday.

A silent moment of recollection,

the holding back of a tear.

An acceptance of who I am

And not who I was,

All I want is all you have.

Polo Day

The green lawn of carpet

The sculptured beasts of hell

Riders thundering towards us

Lowly mensen.

Behind fences I sip champagne

And contemplate,

My country's future leaders.

Everyone Should See This Bed

Everyone should see this bed
Where hope falters and
Heroes are welcomed
And praised
That right was done.

Where hands are held
And memories are hurriedly
Remembered
When all he wants to do
Is look forward
Not back.

Where the whiteness of sheets
Almost promise to heal
And all that intensity of love
In one room
Is known to fail.

Closet racists

Closet racists wait and only come out,
When their words safety holds no doubt.
Soapy poison bubbles floating around,
Opinion clouded, above the ground.
I don't see you as black they confess
And yet choosing the orange for the ripeness,
The pith, the juice, peel, pips, I express
Sorrow at such, sudden, colour blindness.

On match days miracles are cardinal.
Amongst veins of stench in the urinal,
Deformed strangers talk cheap disturbing news,
Where it's easy to tell the reds from the blues.
And as floodlights dim the blacks from the whites,
Soon scarves will hang like discarded kites.

Innocent Horizons

Lying in that innocent grass
Sun in one eye, so you squint.
So close to the ground, you count the blades.
It was so innocent, you could pick a blade and taste the day.
Only size 4 and below are allowed,
those who only know the boundaries of this sweet land and nothing else.
Bounded by trees with tempting gaps.
Gaps that tempt the smokers and innocent lovers who know nothing.

Looking across the lop-sided land through one eye,
at the white goal posts with no nets.
Realising that there was nothing to stop your goals.

And on those sweet playing fields,
where we practiced Life's games,
nothing is apparent.
Only that the grass stains don't matter yet and that soon the whistle will be heard

Reading Between The Lines

Whilst all around us, madness reigns.
Visiting families, dates to be kept,
bills to be paid.
Missed birthdays, shrugged shoulders at
missed opportunities.
Was I invited to this I ask?
I wanted days watching my children.
Touching my wife's shoulder on a
Sunday morning,
her asleep, me in wonder.

While the world frowns over papers and
figures
I want to nudge my way past,
away from normality and onto certainty.
Where innocence prevails.

Corrupting The Pure

Imagine if they took all this away today
My wife, my lover, my friend.
Imagine if my children were no longer there,
to ask me nonsensical questions
About the moon during daytime
and staying up after eight.
Imagine if they took all this away
and laughed and said
well, you had it all.
And didn't you know?
That love is retrospective and when
it has nowhere to go,
it erupts from within,
forcing us to see through
infected splinters,
corrupting the pure.

Tales From The Riverbank

Bad memories fade fast.
Only bitterness remains for those

who demand on pocketing images that
we should know

Are worthless.

Those strong summer days
Stretching out amongst immature limbs.

And as you lay, close up to that blade of
grass,

unknowingly placing a perspective on
Life

You ignored that slow, flowing river.
Ignored the strength of the rays on your
shoulders,

only concerned with impression
and expression,

of a soul that was to become You.

They said....

I hadn't thought,
not considered.
Until the bird appeared at my side
and I recalled you were a like a sparrow,

they said.
Our nest was full I guess
and your egg had been broken,
raided by me,
in our rushed wisdom.

I still think of you
through crushed tears.
On reminded days of
almost school books,
and candles in drawers.

If Someone...

If someone were to ask why I love you
I would reply I could not say
Love is not only blind to those that agree its terms
It cushions you to the blow of reason
I could say it is your hair
the way it frames a perfect face
I could site your eyes as being windows
into a mind I can never understand
I may even be as brash as to describe the
incredible innocence of your shoulders
that form on an early morning,
a sculpture so pure.
If someone were to ask me why I stay with you
when words appear as harshly as an
unforeseen thunderstorm
I would say it is written somewhere
that a spark creates a burning fire.
And a flame is preferable to me,
in this short life
and while all around me fools talk of love
mine will remain unspoken
because the soul never speaks
it is left just to wonder,
at the beauty of it all.

A World Turned Upside Down

It kind of smells, the young girl said
As the artists wares were examined.
Might be the materials the mother hopefully adds.
The socialist rustles quietly away
upstairs, unhearing but all knowing
Thoughts of revolutions, discussed over late pints
 masking the reality of real Life

Thoughts scrubbed away with the soap of bills
and food
And unrequited Love.
Simple things in Life are all
The stability of reasoning overcome within
the artist's brightly coloured shack
Coffees shared. Fags lent.
And livelihood gained by selling
Stalinistesque imagery
dressed up as lighthouses
and buckets and spades.

Gasoline Souls

If I'm going down, I'm going down burning.
Inhale this dormant fuel that soaks my clothes.
Stand well back and admire the seeping dark stain
That cloaks my aura and pools at my feet.

If it stings your eyes look away but listen
To the slow grind of flint I hold in my hand
And if I falter, interrupt my stride
I'll grip your hand and take one last breath
Our gasoline souls burning, like a desert sun.

Time Machine

I need to go back in time with a duffel bag
To collect what I had but have now lost.
Laughter with absolute abandonment
Living a day with no plans or maps
Feeling sun on the face and knowing there'll be more
Lying by rivers and hearing breeze and ghostly voices
Evenings that lay ahead like a mystery
The plot not yet written, the characters not cast.
My bag will be full and one by one
I'll take them out and regenerate my perfect self.

The rebirth of Soul

My being started with the Blues
Then my teen years rocked with the Roll
When I met you the challenging Jazz
years began.
Where everything complicates
And life has an edge
And now as my soul is once again reborn
I realise all these parts are me
And I can hear them all with each beat
of the heart,
Each tap of the foot.

Luxembourg

I arrived from nowhere and arrived somewhere.
I left what I didn't understand
and joined what I understood.
I left failed friends behind and
discovered lovers.
I left greyness and found scoops of
green valleys.
I severed what I knew and became what
I am.

The foreign language of Love

I crave you, I don't want to save you.
I want you, not those around you.
I want us to procreate, not procrastinate.
I want us to go fishing and for our lines to cross,
I want us to dive for pearls, not dive for dear life.
I want our kites to soar, with tails trailing,
Glittering, shimmering and proud.

Never See the real Me

Never see the real me
The one that pretends to love
The one that wishes to be someone else

Never see the real me
The one who wants someone else
The one who pretends to care

Never see the real me
Who says I love you
To reassure and lie

Never see the real me
Who sees past your look
And into the arms of another

Never see the real me
With the stone soul
The glazed eyes
The thinning lips.

The Perfect Chord

I'm out of key with this orchestra.
I hear G minors and want to play F sharps.
I'm walking out of beat to their song
and seeing a chorus where the verse should be.
I need to harmonise in thirds with a cello that vibrates with my soul
and not feel that we are back at the start,
rehearsing for confrontation,
the muffled acceptance, before
the podium sounds and the conductor prepares.

www.ingramcontent.com/pod-product-compliance
Lightning Source LLC
Chambersburg PA
CBHW070751050426
42449CB00010B/2419